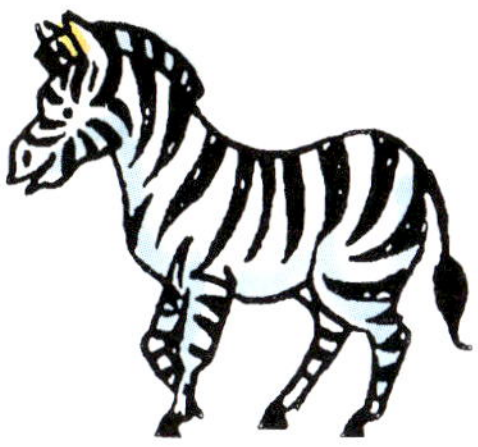

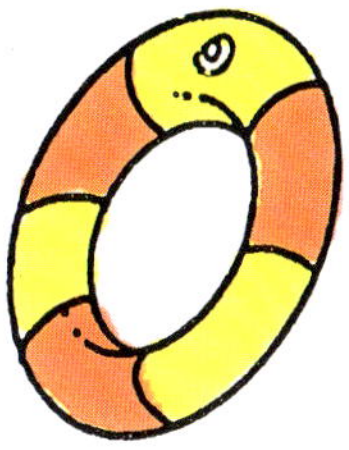
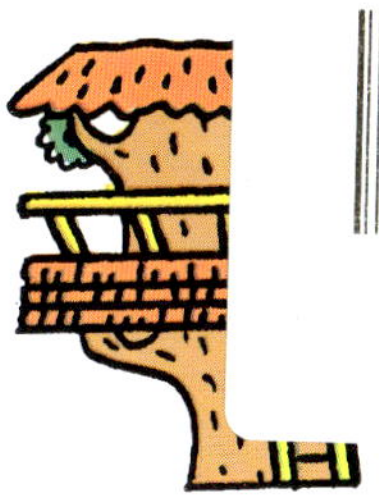

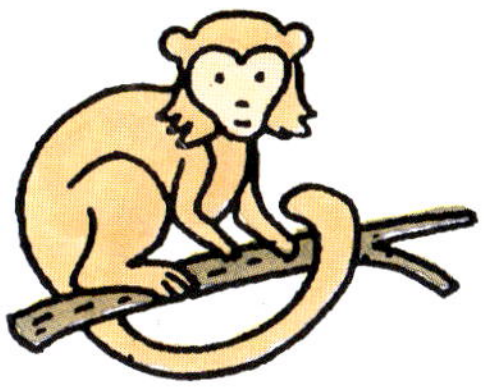
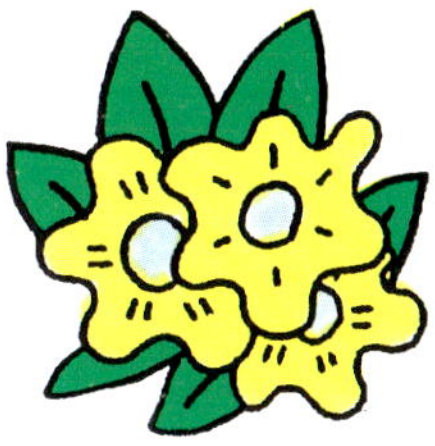

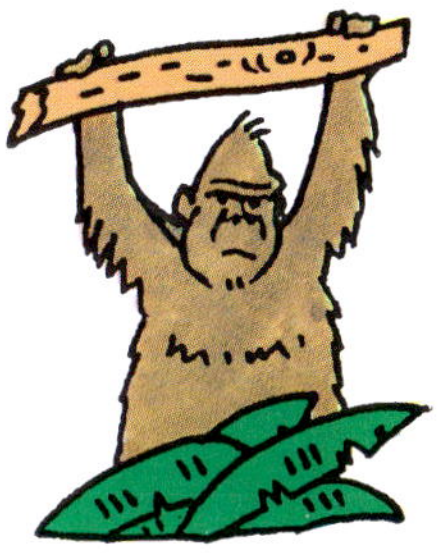
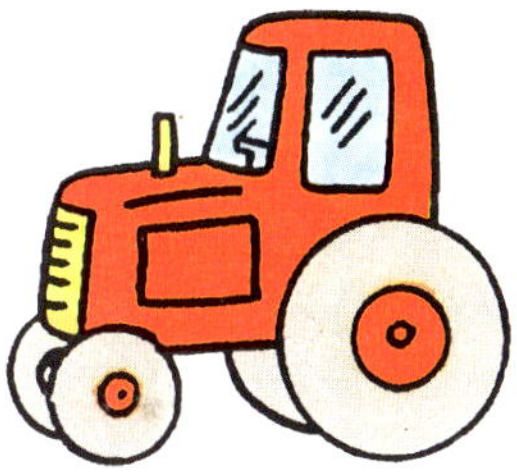
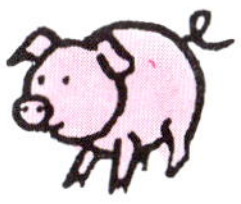
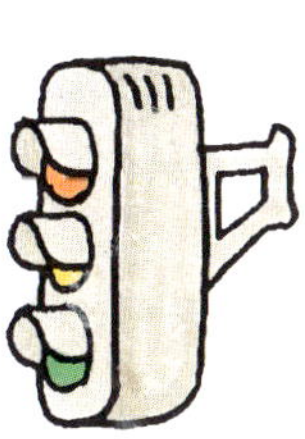
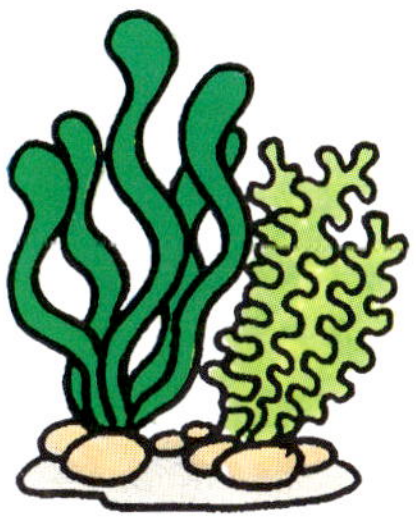
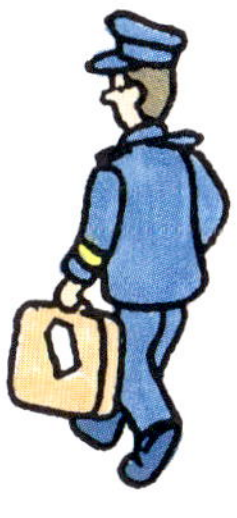
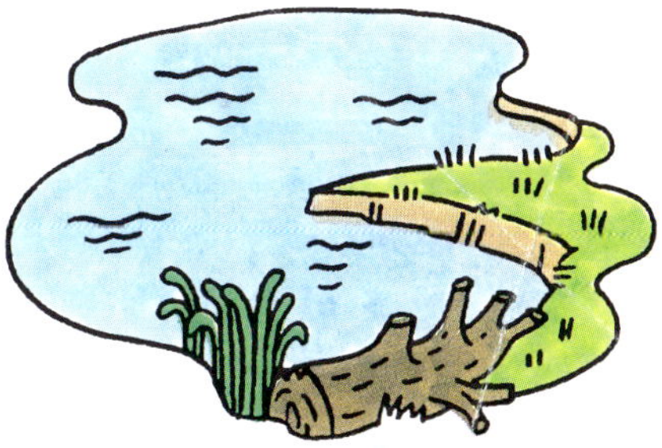

Words and Pictures

How to use this book
a note to parents

This book is designed to encourage your child's development,
putting words and pictures together in a way that makes learning fun.
It will help your child's understanding of the world,
and extend his or her vocabulary and verbal skills.

Share the book with your child, encouraging him or her to recognize
and name objects, and relate what is happening in the pictures to
his or her own experiences. Later, help him or her to
read the words in the margin.

text by Jane Clempner

illustrations by David Moss

Copyright © 1993 Egmont Group
All rights reserved.
Published in Great Britain by World International Publishing Ltd.,
an Egmont Company, Egmont House, PO Box 111,
Great Ducie Street, Manchester M60 3BL.
Printed in Italy.
ISBN 0-7498-1310-5

On the farm

- farmhouse
- trailer
- farmer
- goat
- cow
- calf
- sheep 
- pigsty 
- hay bale 
- apple tree 
- milk tanker 
- geese  
- beehive 
- silo 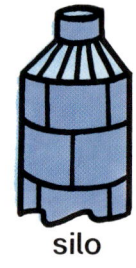
- orchard 
- barn

combine harvester · hen · cockerel · horse · foal

pig

piglet

cat

carrots

dog

wheat · greenhouse · henhouse · water trough · tractor

At the supermarket

mother

yellow bananas

father

money

baby

red apples

one loaf of bread

basket

five tomatoes

cucumber

mushrooms

green grapes

meat

lettuce

shopping list

jars of jam

trolley

four lemons

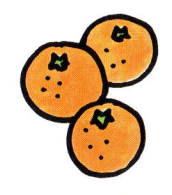

oranges  | two cakes  | pears  | three cans  | wine  | cheese

sign

scales

margarine

milk

carrier bag

breakfast cereals  | sausages  | cashier  | till  | eggs

Beside the sea

sand sandcastle shells crab flippers

swimsuit

seaweed

coolbox

book

beach towel

mask diver ice cream beach ball sunshade

sea   yacht   wind-break   water skier   speedboat

fishing net

shorts

armbands

windsurfer

pedalo   fish   sunglasses   bucket   swimming ring

The harbour

ferry fishing boat rowing boat tug boat

cargo ship

rope

fisherman

buoy

fishing rod

ticket office oars sailor fishing net lifejacket sail

dinghy raft oil tanker

lighthouse

cargo

seagulls

lifebelt

fork lift truck

captain

passengers jetty crane fish anchor

In the classroom

teacher

toilet

boy

wash basin

girl

soap dispenser

map

chair

paper towel

table

clay

bricks

radiator

book

bookcase

ruler

computer

picture	clock	paintbrushes	sand tray	waste bin	mirror

plant

height chart

paints

pencils

easel

crayons	measuring jug	scissors	apron	glue	jigsaw

The adventure playground

swing

jumper

see-saw

coat

slide

sandpit

pushchair

climbing frame

grandma

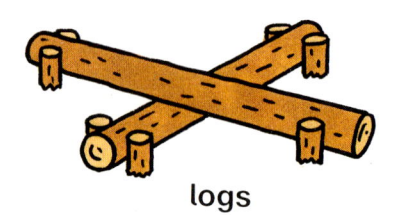

logs

roller skates

bench

tree

balloon

tyre grandad rope bridge litter bin

skipping rope

sandwiches

safety helmet

tunnel

bicycle

pond scarf skateboard duck

In the city

- toy shop
- bakery
- café
- police car
- telephone box
- window cleaner
- optician
- statue
- taxi
- train
- cinema
- motorcycle
- florist
- petrol pump
- cash machine

bus crossing bicycle traffic lights fire engine

lorry

offices

car

street lamp

supermarket   bank   car park   service station   umbrella

In the countryside

cottage

mountain

rucksack

cloud

canoe

walking boots

forest

fox

hedgehog

map

deer

lamb

stream

squirrel

bridge

picnic table   butterfly   bird   swan

lake

saucepan

church

kettle

village

barbecue   waterfall   flowers   footpath   tent

The building site

bricks

house

bulldozer

tipper truck

bricklayer

garage

sand

cement

timber

cement mixer

ladder

carpenter

window frame

painter

door

digger

mortar

dumper truck · scaffolding · electric drill · plans · shovel · pick · pipes · hammer · screwdriver · hard hat · saw · saw bench · trowel · water hose · roof tiles · site cabin · road roller · wheelbarrow · architect

On the move

stairs

bookshop

check-in desk

van

radar

café

drinks machine

clock

arrow

coach

customs officers

newspaper

traffic signals

cleaner

x-ray machine	timetable	conveyor belt	pilot	luggage

- wind sock
- control tower
- flag
- runway
- jet engine
- fuel tanker

escalator	aircraft	information desk

On safari

- jeep
- zebra
- chameleon
- lion cub
- rhinoceros
- guide
- turtle
- hat
- antelope
- binoculars
- video camera
- lion  
- hippopotamus 
- viewing platform 
- camera 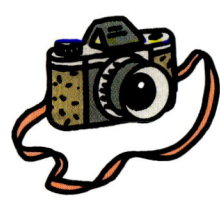
- monkey

chimpanzee | lioness | termite mounds | tiger | snake

giraffe

parrot

flamingo

gorilla

tourist | crocodile | ostrich | water buffalo | elephant

Out in space

- moon landing craft
- space station
- satellite
- spaceship
- visor
- stars
- crater
- Earth
- moon rocks
- shooting star
- flag
- telescope
- observatory
- engines
- camera
- satellite dish

space helmet | Sun | space shuttle | moon buggy

aerial

volcano

space pack

lifeline

solar panels | moon boots | astronaut | planet

Word list

aerial
aircraft
anchor
antelope
apple tree
apples
apron
architect
armbands
arrow
astronaut

baby
bakery
balloon
bananas
bank
barbecue
barn
basket
beach ball
beach towel
beehive
bench
bicycle
binoculars
bird
book
bookcase
bookshop
boy
bread
breakfast cereals
bricklayer
bricks
bridge
bucket
bulldozer
buoy
bus
butterfly

café
cakes
calf
camera
canoe

cans
captain
car
car park
cargo
cargo ship
carpenter
carrier bag
carrots
cash machine
cashier
cat
cement
cement mixer
chair
chameleon
check-in desk
cheese
chimpanzee
church
cinema
clay
cleaner
climbing frame
clock
cloud
coach
coat
cockerel
combine harvester
computer
control tower
conveyor belt
coolbox
cottage
cow
crab
crane
crater
crayons
crocodile
crossing
cucumber
customs officers

deer
digger
dinghy
diver

dog
door
drinks machine
duck
dumper truck

Earth
easel
eggs
electric drill
elephant
engines
escalator

farmer
farmhouse
father
ferry
fire engine
fish
fisherman
fishing boat
fishing net
fishing rod
five
flag
flamingo
flippers
florist
flowers
foal
footpath
forest
fork lift truck
four
fox
fuel tanker

garage
geese
giraffe
girl
glue
goat
gorilla
grandad
grandma
grapes
green

greenhouse
guide

hammer
hard hat
hat
hay bale
hedgehog
height chart
hen
henhouse
hippopotamus
horse
house

ice cream
information desk

jars of jam
jeep
jet engine
jetty
jigsaw
jumper

kettle

ladder
lake
lamb
lemons
lettuce
lifebelt
lifejacket
lifeline
lighthouse
lion
lion cub
lioness
litter bin
loaf
logs
lorry
luggage

map
margarine
mask
measuring jug